921
NEW

c.1

Schultz, Pearle
Henriksen.

Isaac Newton:
scientific genius

DATE		
Alexis Baul~~~~~		

Isaac
NEWTON
SCIENTIFIC GENIUS

own about discovering the earth's diurnal motion. In order therto I will consider
ye earth's diurnal motion alone without ye annual, that having little influence
on ye experiment I shall here propound. Suppose then BDG represents
the Globe of ye earth carried round once a day about its center C
from west to east according to ye order of ye letters BDG; & let
A be a heavy body suspended in the Air & moving round with
the earth so as perpetually to hang over ye same point
thereof B. Then imagin this body B let fall & its
gravity will give it a new motion towards ye center of ye
earth without diminishing ye old one from west to east.
Whence the motion of this body from west to east, by reason
that before it fell it was more distant from ye center of
ye earth then the parts of ye earth at wch it arrives in its
fall, will be greater then the motion from west to east of ye parts of ye
earth at wch ye body arrives in its fall: & therefore it will not descend
ye perpendicular AC, but outrunning ye parts of ye earth will shoot forward to ye east side of the perpendicular . . . . ing in its fall a spiral line ADEC.
quite contrary to ye opi . . . . that if ye earth moved,
heavy bodies in falling . . . . fall on ye west side of
ye perpendicular. . . . . perpendicular eastward
will in a descent of . . . . & yet I am apt
to think it may . . . . Suppose then
in a very cal . . . . silk line from
the top of a . . . . small hole made
in a plate of . . . . ding or Well &
ye ye bullet . . . . water so as to
. . . . . from . . . . steel lying . . . .
& south to . . . . stand in æquilibr . . .
but yet with . . . . decline to ye
west side of . . . . The steel being
so placed und . . . . to ye top of th
fall by cutti . . . . fall constant
on ye east . . . . of ye earth
But what if . . . . mpt to try
it. If any . . . . my
opinion wou . . . . he windows
being fir . . . . bly may
be apt to . . . . of ye
Well. it . . . . be
would . . . . greatly
a y . . . . its
on . . . . rough

Isaac
NEWTON
SCIENTIFIC GENIUS

by Pearle and Harry Schultz

illustrated by Cary

GARRARD PUBLISHING COMPANY
Champaign, Illinois

Dedicated to the

MEN OF APOLLO

"One small step for a man—

One giant leap for mankind."

Picture credits:

Bettmann Archive: p. 1

Culver Pictures: p. 10

National Portrait Gallery, London: pp. 2, 140

Picture Collection, New York Public Library: pp. 60 (both), 96 (top)

Radio Times Hulton Picture Library: pp. 24, 40, 52, 70, 86, 90, 110, 113, 121, 128, 134

Trinity College Library, Cambridge, England: p. 96 (bottom)

Contents

1. A Child Born on Christmas Day

The full moon sailed high in the winter sky, lighting the frosty fields and the marshes along the river. Moonlight brightened the cluster of thatched cottages tucked away in the little valley and the two-story manor house close by.

It was Christmas Day 1642, and hours yet before dawn. Inside the old stone farmhouse called Woolsthorpe Manor in Lincolnshire, England, one room glowed with candlelight. A newborn baby lay in a hooded cradle pulled up to the warmth of the fire blazing on the open hearth.

England was engaged in a great Civil War. King Charles' army was fighting an army led by Oliver Cromwell, a member of Parliament, to decide who would rule England. Night patrols from both sides ranged the countryside, and once darkness fell, cautious folk seldom left their cottages. Two neighbor women, however, had come to help at this baby's birth.

They spoke softly to each other.

"'Tis said a baby born on Christmas Day is gifted with rare powers," one whispered.

"Aye," the older woman agreed. "I've heard that said. But Widow Newton was not expecting this baby for some weeks yet. He is scarcely strong enough to cry."

Her companion nodded. "Still, to be born on Christmas Day is surely a sign of God's favor," she said. "A son will be such a comfort to Mrs. Newton, with the poor soul's husband dead these past three months."

The woman in the great bed at the far end of the room stirred. The two neighbors hurried to Hannah Newton's side and placed the baby in her arms.

The new mother looked down at the little bundle. "Truly, the baby is small enough to fit into a quart pot," Hannah Newton marveled. She would name the child Isaac after his father, she decided.

One week later, on New Year's Day, Isaac Newton was baptized. Wrapped in layers of clothes, the baby was carried to the parish church across River Witham for his christening. Recorded in the parish register of Colsterworth Church under the heading of "baptisms" is the entry:

Isaac sonne of Isaac and Hanna Newton
Jan. 1

Spring came early in 1643, bringing mild weather. Troops from both sides of England's Civil War launched new offensives.

Managing the manor farm was difficult for Hannah Newton during these hard times. There was no money to hire the help needed to farm the land and protect the crops from the soldiers. As in the past, some fields were rented to tenant farmers. This income, however, was barely enough to support her little family.

There were other worries too. The roof needed repair, and the stone walls around the courtyard were crumbling.

To see the manor in such a rundown condition troubled Hannah Newton. The property had been a wedding gift from the Newton family. Unfortunately, she and her husband had never had money enough to manage it properly.

First things first, Hannah Newton reminded herself. She would trust in God and not worry about the repairs for Woolsthorpe Manor until her son grew stronger.

Woolsthorpe Manor, where Isaac Newton was born and grew to manhood

After all, hadn't the clergyman who baptized the child reminded her that a son born after his father's death would have good fortune? Such children were always unusual, the rector had said.

However, neither hopeful rector nor loving mother ever dreamed how rare a mind would grow inside that tiny head.

The frail Christmas baby of Woolsthorpe Manor would one day become the scientist whose work influenced human thought for centuries to come. And 1642 would be marked in history as the year that the world lost the greatness of Galileo and gained the genius of Isaac Newton.

2. The Lincolnshire Lad

Hannah Newton was discouraged. The Civil War still raged throughout Lincolnshire. Bands of soldiers came pounding on her door at all hours, seeking food or horses.

"Managing the manor in times like these is impossible for a woman," Grandmother Ayscough declared. She and Hannah's brother James had come for a winter visit.

"You should remarry, Hannah," she announced firmly. "Your brother has heard from the Reverend Barnabas Smith of North Witham. He has made you a fine offer of marriage!"

Hannah listened uneasily. The clergyman her mother spoke of was a wealthy sixty-three-year-old bachelor.

"Reverend Smith's offer is generous, Hannah," her brother began. "He will both repair and enlarge Woolsthorpe Manor. Also, some farmland he owns will be deeded to Isaac. The income from that property, plus the rental of the Woolsthorpe fields, will support the boy amply."

James avoided his sister's eyes. "However, the clergyman is not accustomed to small children. Isaac must remain behind to live at Woolsthorpe."

Hannah Newton gasped.

James hurried on, "Our mother could live here and look after Isaac for you. North Witham is not so far from here. You'd see your son often."

Hannah was silent. There were so many things to consider. Much as she hated to leave Isaac, it seemed that this new marriage was the best solution to many problems.

Details were soon arranged, and Hannah Newton moved to her new husband's home in the rectory at North Witham. Her puzzled three-year-old son was left behind at Woolsthorpe.

"Your mother will come home to visit soon, Isaac," his grandmother promised. "Why, just a fortnight or two and we'll be seeing her again, lad."

The visits were little comfort. His mother would come home only to disappear again.

By the time Isaac was nine, his mother had two more children. But what good was there, Isaac wondered, in having a half-sister and a half-brother? Little Mary was much too timid to play with him. And as for Benjamin! Isaac scowled. Benjamin was a mere baby!

Besides, he and the other children lived in different houses. They were not at all like ordinary brothers and sisters. Isaac stared out the manor house window and sighed. If only he had a real friend to play with.

His sigh reached Grandmother Ayscough's ears. She went to the window to see what Isaac was watching. In a nearby field the sons of the tenant cottagers were playing a wild game of soldiers. Each boy flourished a wooden stick for a sword.

After years of Civil War, King Charles' Royal Army had been defeated in 1645. The king himself had been removed from the throne and beheaded. His place as ruler was taken by Cromwell, who was given the title of lord protector. Although the Civil War was over, country lads still played soldiers.

Isaac read her thoughts. "They asked me to join them, grandmother, but I don't like mock battles. Besides, I'm too small for their rough games," he added truthfully.

Left to himself, young Isaac Newton found his own pleasures. Nearby were fields to roam and marshes to explore. His natural curiosity took him in all directions. He gathered herbs for his grandmother, picked wild flowers to dry for his own collection, and selected shiny pebbles to arrange on his bedroom shelf. On Sunday mornings he walked with grandmother to church.

Summer days were best of all. There was so much to see and think about.

Lying quietly at the edge of a pond, Isaac observed water spiders skating on the surface of the little stream behind the manor house. How strange that they did not sink nor seem to wet their feet!

Sometimes flocks of waterfowl dotted the sky above the Colsterworth marshes. Isaac marveled at the sight. How great God was to have created so wonderful a world! Isaac sketched the birds, using charcoal and scraps of paper for his pictures.

When winter came, Isaac walked alone across the fields every morning to the village school. If his work interested him, Isaac was a good student. When he found the lessons dull, he escaped into the world of his imagination.

Although he could do arithmetic problems in his head, Isaac was not the schoolmaster's favorite pupil. "Always asking questions, that one is," the teacher complained.

On winter evenings, seated by the kitchen fire, grandmother told stories. Isaac whittled little models while his grandmother talked. He handled tools well, and he liked the feel of the wood.

Isaac's model toys were always constructed with working parts: wheels turned, windmill sails moved, and tiny gears meshed together.

One night Grandmother Ayscough watched the pocketknife flash up and down. "What are you making, Isaac?" she asked.

"A new toy waterwheel," he answered. "My last one did not work. The wheel moved sluggishly. I won't make that mistake again, grandmother. These parts are smaller and will allow space for the wood to swell when it gets water-soaked."

In the year 1653, Isaac Newton's world turned upside down again. He was eleven now and almost through school. Grandmother told him the startling news. "Barnabas Smith is dead. Your mother is coming home again," she said.

Isaac's heart thumped. How many times had he wished that his stepfather would die? Again and again during the lonely years he had said the words to himself. But he had not really meant it.

"Your mother is coming home to Woolsthorpe!" Grandmother Ayscough repeated.

Isaac nodded. Mother was coming home. With her, no doubt, would come six-year-old Mary, two-year-old Benjamin, and baby Hannah.

Grandmother Ayscough guessed at his thoughts. Well-a-day! So the boy was jealous of the small children. "Your mother could scarcely leave them behind in North Witham. Now could she?"

Isaac stared gloomily at her.

3. Meet Miss Storey

One day not long after Mrs. Smith's return, Isaac's Uncle William came to call. The Reverend William Ayscough had been educated at Cambridge University. Now he thought Isaac should be sent away to a good school.

"Isaac has almost finished school," Hannah Smith objected.

"Bah! Those little village schools teach farm boys to trace their names and read a Bible verse. Isaac will need more than that to manage a place as large as Woolsthorpe when he grows up. King's School at Grantham—that's the place for our Isaac," Uncle William insisted.

Grantham, six miles to the north, was an important market town in Lincolnshire. It was famous for King's School, founded long ago by England's Henry VIII.

Isaac's heart sank when his mother told him. "Do I need more school? Why go all the way to Grantham?" he asked.

I belong here at Woolsthorpe, Isaac was thinking. Here where the marshy fens are just right for summer exploring. Here where I can lie near the hearth on winter afternoons and dream of—

A guilty feeling troubled him. Mother was always telling him there was no place for daydreaming on a busy farm. Was she sending him away to cure him of his lazy habit?

Isaac asked, "Where could I live, mother? I know nobody in Grantham."

"I do, Isaac." Hannah Smith was smiling now. "I know the Clarks, a family living not far from King's School. Mrs. Clark and I were childhood friends. She wrote me that you can board with them."

So mother had already made plans! Isaac scowled.

Hannah Smith continued, "Mrs. Clark is married to an apothecary."

Isaac felt sudden interest. Apothecaries worked with chemicals and herbs. Perhaps Mr. Clark would let him help in the apothecary shop.

"I'd want to take my little mechanical models along," he warned his mother. "Would there be room for them at the Clarks?"

There would be space for everything he treasured, his mother promised. The Clarks had a fine garret room all ready for him.

"They have one child, Mrs. Clark's daughter by her first marriage," Hannah Smith explained. "I think Catherine Storey is about your age. Perhaps you'll become good friends."

Isaac made a face. Girls! Girls broke hammers and lost nails and were afraid of mice. Isaac determined to have nothing to do with this one.

Catherine, however, was counting the days until Isaac arrived. When the farm cart that carried Isaac to Grantham reached the Clarks' house, she was there to greet him.

"I'm glad you're here, Isaac," Catherine said merrily. "I'll help carry your things up to your room." While their mothers visited together, Isaac and Catherine hauled boxes and bundles down from the cart and up to the attic room.

"Are you glad you're going to school here? Is the room all right?" Catherine bubbled over with questions.

Isaac surveyed his surroundings shyly. Everything was clean and orderly. There were shelves to hold his clothes. The narrow bed was covered with a cheerful red quilt. Before the shuttered window was a large oak table. What a grand place at which to work!

Isaac sighed with relief. There was ample space here for his precious models. Perhaps he could even begin new collections of minerals and dried wild flowers.

Carefully, he unwrapped his bundle of tools. Out came a pocketknife, a small hatchet, the new hammer, some wood pegs, and a few nails. He arranged them in order on the table. Catherine's eyes sparkled. Here was someone to repair her toy furniture!

It was the start of the first real friendship in Isaac Newton's life.

"I like living with the Clarks," he admitted to

his mother a few weeks later. Mrs. Smith had come up to Grantham with the last of the vegetables for market.

Hannah Smith smiled at her son. "I knew you'd like them. Mr. Clark tells me that you enjoy the apothecary shop too."

Isaac's eyes shone. How could he ever describe the wonders of Mr. Clark's shop? There, on shelves reaching from floor to ceiling, were bottles filled with colored powders, strangely named liquids, and exciting chemicals. Fragrant odors wafted from earthenware jars of herbs and vials of medicinal oils.

"I know some of the names already, mother— flowers of sulphur, belladonna, balsam of Mecca. Wait till I show you the notebook I've begun!"

"I can see you get along well with the Clarks," Mrs. Smith said. "Tell me how you are progressing in school."

Isaac's happy mood vanished. School—that was another story.

Young Isaac Newton was a reluctant scholar at King's School in Grantham.

4. The King's School Scholar

Isaac stared out the arched windows while the schoolmaster's voice droned on. The Latin lesson seemed endless. Mr. Stokes, the headmaster himself, would be coming to teach Bible history next. All afternoon there would be more classes—logic and grammar, ancient history, mathematics, and penmanship.

Isaac sighed. He had meant to study Latin last night. Instead, he had read an old book of astronomy until the candle burned down to nothing. Such wonderful old books he had found stored in the Clark's dusty attic: astronomy, botany, chemistry, anatomy.

"Newton!" The Latin master's voice pounced at him.

Isaac bent over his book, but his thoughts were elsewhere. If Headmaster Stokes does not keep us past noon, he was thinking, I can run home. I'll mark my sundial and be back before logic class.

Mr. Clark was allowing Isaac to chart the sunshine's daily path across the south wall of the Clark house. Pegs pounded into the wall marked shadow patterns cast by the sun at early morning, midday, and late afternoon. Isaac observed with interest that the sun reached different heights at noon, depending on the season of the year.

When school was over that day, Dr. Clark, the mathematics master, visited his brother, the apothecary. He wanted to talk about Isaac.

"The boy shows little interest in his studies," Dr. Clark said with concern. "His progress is poor, and he's made no friends."

The teacher picked up Isaac's notebook from the table near the apothecary's big mortar and pestle. "You fill his mind too full of chemistry, brother. Of what use to him is this knowledge of chemicals and drugs?"

The apothecary sighed. It was true that Isaac was more interested in the apothecary laboratory than in his lessons. But the boy had such an inquiring mind! Why, even now he was over at the Gunnerby Road, observing workmen build a new windmill.

"Come and see Isaac's room," Mr. Clark suggested. "There is something I want to show you."

The two men climbed to the attic chamber. Dr. Clark stared in wonder at Isaac's charcoal drawings, which covered one entire wall. "Birds, beasts, men, ships . . . and all very well designed," he muttered. "Here he has sketched intricate plans for a sundial."

The schoolmaster studied the mechanical models on Isaac's shelves. "Why, these are no mere toys. See these small gears. Did he whittle these himself?"

"All this is Isaac's work," the apothecary said. "The boy has a passion to construct things that move."

The apothecary pointed to a half-finished doll's chest. "That's a gift for Catherine's birthday. Next he has promised to make us a water clock. He says that water slowly dripping on a block of wood attached with string to the hour hand will make the clock run."

A clock! Few people were rich enough to possess a clock. Dr. Clark stared at his brother in disbelief.

Following the mathematics master's visit, Isaac made an effort to improve at school. However, there were so many interesting things to do that his good intentions soon vanished. In a strange book called *Mysteries of Nature and Art*, Isaac found directions for making simple fireworks and watercolor paints. He copied these things into his growing notebook.

As time went on, Isaac made a water clock, a small wheelchair with hand controls, and a working model of the Gunnerby Road windmill. Every part of Isaac's mill was carefully whittled to scale. Each shaft and gear fitted together properly. Small white sails completed the model.

"Go outside and look up on your housetop!" Isaac told the Clarks one day.

Fastened to the roof was Isaac's model windmill. Its little sails were filled with wind and whirled round and round. The Clarks cheered.

Next Isaac placed the windmill on the floor inside the house. Slowly the sails began to move.

"There's no wind in here," puzzled Mr. Clark. "What makes the mill go? Isaac, how have you done this trick?"

"No trick, Mr. Clark. It's mouse power. See?" Isaac opened the tiny door of the mill to show him a small mouse inside a little treadwheel. The astonished apothecary roared with laughter.

No one laughed, however, the night Isaac terrified the countryside with his lantern. As a surprise for Catherine, Isaac built a large paper kite. One dark evening he attached a glowing lantern to the kite and launched it forth. Catherine shouted happily as the flickering light dipped and soared through the night skies above them. Nearby countryfolk were terrified out of their wits. They thought the strange light was a comet sent by God to warn them of coming disaster.

Not long after the kite episode, something that Isaac would remember all his life happened to him on his way to school. A big bully who sat next to Isaac in class knocked him down and kicked him.

The savage kick was painful, but the insult to

Isaac's pride hurt even more. When classes for the day were over, the humiliated Isaac challenged the bigger boy to a fight.

Their schoolmates jeered. What? Young Newton fight?

The bully laughed too—right in Isaac's face. Isaac exploded with anger. Moments later the bigger boy was on the ground being thrashed.

Isaac's successful encounter with the bully also marked the beginning of his success in school. For the first time in his life he wanted to study. He was determined to get ahead of his tormentor in schoolwork too.

"No more daydreaming," he vowed. He turned to his books with new concentration. Each night the candle burned late in his attic bedroom. Mathematics, especially, interested him now.

Several months later, the headmaster greeted Isaac with a wide smile. "Come to my office," he said. "I know something that should please you."

At noon recess Isaac ran all the way home. Triumphant, he shouted the news to Catherine. He was not just top boy in class, but top scholar of King's School!

5. "He'll Be No Farmer"

"I wish you weren't leaving, Isaac," Catherine said. She stood in the attic doorway, watching Isaac pack for the trip back to Woolsthorpe. It had been such a wonderful four years.

Isaac tied up the last bundle. There! Books, models, clothes..., everything was ready.

"I must go home, Catherine," he explained again. "Mother needs me on the farm. My half-brother is too young to help, and we can't find enough men to hire these days."

Life in Cromwell's commonwealth had proved to be far from pleasant. Taxes continued to be high, and living costs had soared. English people wondered whether they had killed their king only to find new tyranny under the Lord Protector and his Puritan army. Cromwell's troops were everywhere—controlling worship in the churches, education in the schools, and justice in the courts.

"Mother is depending on me," Isaac continued. "Besides, she says it's time I learned about farming."

Catherine shook her head. "I just can't see you as a farmer."

Isaac laughed. "Woolsthorpe will be mine someday, you know. After all, Catherine, I'm nearly sixteen years old."

Isaac had grown very fond of the Clarks, and saying good-bye was difficult.

"The clock is for you, Mrs. Clark," Isaac reminded Catherine's mother. "Remember to put the proper amount of water in it every morning."

Mr. Clark grasped his hand in farewell. "Keep up your notebooks, Isaac," the apothecary said. "Keep learning."

Catherine was crying, Isaac noticed. "It isn't really good-bye," he told her. "I'll be coming to market for mother quite often. I'll stop to see you every time."

Now that Isaac had returned to Woolsthorpe, his days were busy with farm chores: watching Woolsthorpe's flocks of woolly sheep, plowing the rich Lincolnshire earth, and harvesting the grain. Meat must be salted for winter use. Farm animals must be cared for. And Isaac must learn how to bargain and sell farm produce at Grantham market.

Isaac went to bed weary each night. There was so much to learn!

All too soon Hannah Newton Smith began to wonder if it had been wise to bring Isaac home from school. "He really tries," she told herself, "but did ever a young farmer do so badly?" Too much salt in the winter meat, too little seed in the spring-plowed earth—

In August he had even broken the barn doors. Actually, it was a great wind that had wrecked the doors, but it was Isaac who forgot to latch them. Hannah found him jumping near the barn, happily experimenting with the force of the wind. He found out that if he leaped in the right direction with relation to the wind, he could jump higher.

"There he was, jumping," Hannah Smith told Grandmother Ayscough later, "while the barn doors and shutters all ripped from their hinges!"

"Give the boy time to think like a farmer," Isaac's grandmother advised. "Remember, Isaac has been a scholar for the past four years."

Even a scholar should know enough to shut farm gates. On the days that Isaac forgot, the sheep strayed away to the neighbors' fields.

"That young Newton!" the shepherd exclaimed. "He'll be no farmer. He's only good for school."

Things like this worried Isaac's mother. One day she looked out the window and saw Isaac coming back from Grantham market, leading his horse. "Did he go lame on you, son?" she asked.

Isaac stopped, stared at the horse, and began to laugh. "No, mother, nothing's wrong with the horse. I dismounted outside Grantham to let the horse walk more easily up the steep hill. I forgot to get on again, it seems."

"Oh, Isaac!"

"Well, I was thinking of something else, mother. I made up a fascinating secret code, based entirely on mathematics!"

That was the trouble, Hannah knew. Isaac's mind was everywhere but on farming. Since his return home, the boy had filled two notebooks with ideas and sketches: calendars, geometry problems, astronomy tables, and drawings of birds. Yet he couldn't shoe a horse properly!

"He's dawdled and daydreamed for two years," Mrs. Smith finally confided to her brother William. "Woolsthorpe Manor will go to rack and ruin under Isaac's care, unless he changes."

"Let us be honest with each other, Hannah," the Reverend William Ayscough said to his sister. "Isaac does not purposely neglect his duties here. The boy simply has little desire to be a farmer."

"What will become of him?" Hannah was frightened now. "His father was a farmer, and so was his grandfather before that."

"Isaac loves knowledge," her brother answered thoughtfully. "The Clarks tell me he stops every week on the way to market and reads in their garret."

Hannah nodded. "Isaac enjoys visiting with Catherine."

"It is more than that. It appears that God has

made Isaac to be a scholar, perhaps even a minister. We must make special plans for such a lad. First he should return to King's School and study there another year. By next June he'll be ready to enter Cambridge University."

Hannah was speechless. Cambridge University! "Money would be a great problem," she gasped.

"I have already talked things over with the headmaster at King's School," her brother said. "We both feel certain that Isaac has a good chance of getting a scholarship at Cambridge. Indeed, Mr. Stokes is so eager for the return of his brilliant mathematics student that he agrees to ask no tuition of you now."

And so, in the autumn of 1660, Isaac returned to King's School in Grantham. Woolsthorpe Manor settled down to normal again under the capable management of Hannah Smith.

6. At Cambridge University

The following June, Isaac waved farewell to his mother once more. Down the green lanes rolled the coach on its way to Cambridge, fifty-five miles to the south. Isaac climbed to the top bench, to sit high up in the warm sunshine.

What would it be like at Cambridge University? he wondered. The great university with its many colleges was famous throughout the world. He would be a student at Trinity College. The Reverend William Ayscough had arranged everything for his eighteen-year-old nephew.

Trinity was a royal college founded by Henry VIII, his uncle had explained. It flew the king's standard and was endowed with royal lands. Now that Cromwell had died and King Charles II was on the throne, the college was once again a truly royal institution. The Master of Trinity, as a matter of fact, was appointed by the king himself.

Soon he would be a Trinity man, Isaac thought with deep pride.

The following afternoon the coach clattered into Cambridge and stopped at the White Lion Tavern. Carrying his package of clothing and his father's Bible, Isaac set out to find his college.

The narrow streets of Cambridge town were full of people—merchants, housewives, farmfolk, and students. Tempting odors of roasted meats and fruit pies drifted out of the shops. From all directions came the calls of vendors selling their wares.

"Fish! Fresh fish!"

"Oranges! Who'll buy oranges?"

Isaac was bewildered. "Which way to Trinity College?" he asked a fellow pushing a pastry cart.

The muffin-man jingled his bell and pointed down a little lane. Isaac hurried on. Suddenly there was Trinity's Great Gate, looking just as his uncle had described it!

Isaac paused and gazed soberly up at the statue of King Henry VIII carved above the arched gateway. Woolsthorpe seemed a thousand miles away now. Heart thudding with excitement, Isaac hurried through the passageway.

"Each college is governed by a number of Fellows and the Master," Uncle William had said. "As soon as you arrive, present yourself to Dr. Ferne, the Master of Trinity. Go straight across the courtyard to the Master's lodge."

Trinity College at Cambridge, 1690

Henry Ferne answered Isaac's knock with a hearty welcome. "Come in," he said. "The clerk is registering our new scholars."

"I am Isaac Newton from Woolsthorpe in Lincolnshire, sir."

"Newton from Lincolnshire, eh?" The Master consulted his notes. "Ah, yes—son of Hannah Smith, widow."

Scratch, scratch went the clerk's quill pen, recording the information in the college book for June 5, 1661.

"Your tutor will be Senior Fellow Benjamin Pulleyn," Ferne remarked. "He will advise you about studies and direct your reading."

The clerk whispered something to the Master.

Dr. Ferne continued, "I am reminded that you are to be a sizar, so as to help your mother pay your college expenses. Do you understand the duties, Newton?"

Isaac nodded. Sizars were poor scholars who ran the errands, did chores, and served suppers to their tutors.

"Well, then," said Dr. Ferne, "the next thing is to get yourself settled in chambers."

Following the Master's directions, Isaac found the way to his own quarters. He glanced shyly at his new roommate, who stood talking with some richly dressed young men.

"Is this the cabinet where I put my clothes?" Isaac asked.

The roommate nodded, staring at the dusty bundle Isaac carried. His own fine garments had arrived in proper boxes on a special coach.

"We're just on our way to the tavern," he said. "Will you join us, Newton?"

Isaac shook his head. "Thank you, no. I want to see the library while it is still daylight."

The young men gathered in the doorway burst out laughing. The library! That dusty old building?

Isaac felt their curious eyes examining him. He glanced down at his country-style shoes and carefully mended cloak.

"Another time, perhaps," someone murmured.

Isaac watched the jolly group saunter down the street. How could they waste their time so foolishly? He hurried off in the opposite direction.

Never would Isaac Newton forget the thrill of his first visit to Trinity's Nevile Library. Books and manuscripts were neatly arranged in great wooden bookcases called "classes." Isaac had not dreamed so many books existed in the whole world.

All of them were his to study! Isaac walked humbly up and down the silent aisles.

That night he wrote to his mother. "Like all undergraduates," he reported, "I will study Greek, logic, religion, rhetoric, and mathematics."

It was disappointing that his courses would include no science. English universities, his tutor Pulleyn had explained, began long ago as small religious communities. They still served mainly as centers of education for the clergymen of the Church of England, although many rich young aristocrats also came there for a smattering of culture. Neither Cambridge nor Oxford University offered much in science, then a new subject.

"However, if I do well this first term," Isaac continued in his letter, "I will be allowed to attend some astronomy lectures."

At the beginning Isaac was lonely at college. He felt out of place among the many pleasure-loving Trinity students. Most of them were scornful of his country background.

"Come now, Newton," they teased, "tell us again about the school you attended."

Fuming, Isaac escaped to the quiet library. "It is far easier to deal with ideas and books than with people," he muttered to himself. "Why should they snub me because I didn't prepare for Cambridge at one of their fashionable boarding schools?"

Of all the rowdy Trinity undergraduates, Isaac decided that his roommate was the worst. Night after night their small quarters bulged with his merry companions.

One evening Isaac could stand no more. He hurried from the noisy room to walk in the silence of Trinity's Great Court.

Beside the splashing fountain paced another youth. He introduced himself, "I'm John Wickins. I'm preparing for the ministry."

"I'm Newton. What drives you from your room at this time of night?" Isaac asked.

John Wickins sighed. "A noisy roommate."

Newton's eyes grew thoughtful. "If you agree, Wickins, I see a solution for both of us. I'll ask the clerk of quarters to let us room together. Our fun-loving roommates can share the other chamber."

John Wickins agreed heartily, and the exchange was soon arranged. Isaac moved in with John, bringing with him his belongings, including his many notebooks.

In one notebook Isaac kept a thrifty record of all college expenses. For a long time the entries had been like this:

> a paper book—eight pence
> for a quart bottle and ink to fill it
>   —one shilling seven pence
> a pair of shoestrings—eight pence

Since meeting John, Isaac would sometimes jot down the cost of:

> tennis court
> to town for a custard
> a glass at the tavern with my
>   chamber-fellow

Life at the university was indeed more interesting now that Isaac had found a friend.

An even greater change in Newton's life occurred in 1663. Dr. Isaac Barrow was appointed as the first Lucasian Professor of Mathematics at Trinity.

He would also act as tutor for the more promising students.

"This is good news, John," Isaac told his roommate. "It means that our English universities are finally recognizing the importance of science and mathematics. Barrow is certainly England's greatest living mathematician—"

John interrupted, "He's also a devout Anglican minister. King Charles says he's Britain's finest preacher."

"I think of Barrow as a mathematician and scientist," Isaac insisted. "Those two areas interest me greatly, John. Barrow's specialty is optics, the science of light. How I would like to be accepted as one of Barrow's students!"

When the next vacation came, Isaac took copies of Euclid's *Geometry*, Kepler's *Optics*, and Descartes' *Analytical Geometry* home with him. He intended to be well prepared for Barrow's first lectures.

Tucked inside the crowded book bag were little presents for Catherine and his young sisters and brother at Woolsthorpe. Someday when his education was completed, Isaac thought, he would be marrying Catherine. They had made no promises to each other, but a warm affection had developed between them.

"You are still happy at Cambridge, son?" Hannah Smith asked him that night.

"Oh, mother, Trinity College is a wonderful place," Isaac said. "I could be happy there for the rest of my life—just reading and studying."

Sometimes Catherine wished that Isaac liked university life less. She wondered uneasily about the years ahead. Besides, what good was having Isaac home on vacation when he brought all those books along?

With patient determination, Isaac Newton studied and reviewed. When he returned to Cambridge, he felt confident he would understand Barrow's lectures. Soon after the Easter term began, he was thrilled to learn he had been assigned the new professor as a tutor.

The two looked each other over. Isaac saw a carelessly dressed, stocky man whose long fingers gripped a tobacco pipe. Dr. Barrow was only thirty-three, but he was known in England as a witty scholar and a man of unusual courage.

The professor saw a slim, serious youth of twenty-one with a determined look about him.

"I hear you want to study with me," Barrow said. "We'll waste no time. I'll start you out with some notes I've made on optical lenses. Also, I want to know just how far you have progressed with Descartes' analytics."

"Yes, sir!" Newton felt like shouting.

Under the influence of his great teacher, Isaac Newton was soon investigating every known area of mathematics. The Lucasian Professor realized that the quiet scholar from Lincolnshire was someone very special. "That Newton has a natural talent for mathematics, a rare intuitive skill such as I have never seen. He may soon surpass us all," Dr. Barrow warned the other Fellows.

Days were not long enough for all that Isaac wished to do. Excited by Barrow's lectures on optics, Isaac began grinding small pieces of glass into curved optical lenses.

It felt good to be using his hands again. Soon the lenses were ready for some experiments with rays of sunlight. Next Isaac ground lenses for a simple telescope.

During the winter of 1664–1665, a great comet was traveling across the heavens. Isaac spent hours on a hilltop near the college, huddled in his warmest clothes, watching the night sky. Above him shone the steady moon, the quiet stars, and the glowing comet curving defiantly on its own way.

Night after night Isaac Newton watched and recorded what he saw. He observed the double halo about the moon. He tracked the comet. With all the observational data in his notebooks, why could he not predict this comet's course? Or its position at any given moment in the future? he wondered. There must be a way. But the comet's path was curved; both its speed and its direction changed constantly. No mathematics that Newton knew could solve problems involving such motion.

Isaac searched the works of the world's famous mathematicians. He missed meals and grew ill from lack of sleep, but he would not give up the problem. His mind grappled with the facts, arranging and rearranging his ideas.

Could algebra solve the problem? Geometry? The analytic approach of Descartes? All helped a little, but not enough.

"Well then," Newton decided, "I'll just have to try to create a new system of mathematics."

Several months before his graduation from Cambridge in January 1665, Isaac discovered a mathematical formula for infinite quantities. Using his new equation, Isaac found that he could multiply exceedingly large numbers simply and quickly. This formula is well known today as the *binomial theorem.*

"It's not yet the mathematics to measure the curving path of a comet," Newton admitted to himself. "Still, it can save days—even months—of ordinary multiplication work."

He smiled, feeling good inside. His pleasure in the discovery reminded him of the time he ran all the way home shouting that he was top boy at King's School.

7. The Black Death

Dr. Barrow thrust more wood on the fire and settled back in his chair. "Why aren't you celebrating at the Red Bull Tavern with the other graduates?" he asked his visitor.

Isaac Newton gazed into the leaping flames. It was hard to speak his thoughts, even to Professor Barrow.

This morning at the graduation examinations, why hadn't he felt happier? Wasn't this Bachelor of Arts degree what he had studied and worked for? After three and a half years he would be going home again.

"I need to talk to you, sir," Isaac said at last.

The words poured out. What did Professor Barrow think about his staying on at Trinity to

Dr. Isaac Barrow was a brilliant professor of mathematics and Newton's tutor.

study for a master's degree? There was still so much to learn. He could not bear to leave the university yet.

Dr. Barrow puffed on his pipe and nodded. He believed Isaac's future was at Cambridge. Where else could so bright a mind grow into greatness?

"It is my good fortune to remain here at Trinity a while longer," Isaac wrote his mother later. "I have received scholarship funds that will free me from money worries while I begin work on a master's degree. Dr. Barrow tells me I can hope for a fellowship afterwards, if a vacancy occurs."

Isaac leaned back and read the sentences aloud. How difficult it was to write this letter home!

"The fellowship would give me a generous allowance from college funds, supporting me even beyond the master's degree," he continued. "However, more important than the money is the freedom a fellowship offers. As a Fellow, I'd be allowed to study or do research on my own, on any subject I desired. I would have time to pursue my experiments in optics. With the master's degree completed, I'd probably be expected to tutor students as well."

Isaac placed the quill pen in the holder and stared out the window. Accepting a fellowship meant other things as well—serious things, Dr. Barrow had explained.

Fellowships were open only to those in Holy Orders or those preparing for the ministry. That was stated in the charter rules of the college, set down long ago by the king as head of church and state. Isaac was deeply religious, but did he want to become a clergyman?

"Scientists who aren't independently wealthy usually decide to be ordained," Barrow had told him. "Then they can continue at the university as Fellows, devoting themselves to mathematics and science, and to tutoring as teaching-clergymen."

"It might be simpler to go back home and become a farmer," Isaac had replied.

Barrow had only shaken his head. "You have a passion for science, Newton. Stop worrying about all this now. There are no fellowships vacant anyway. Besides, the Trinity statute about entering Holy Orders hasn't been enforced for years. A newly elected Fellow can postpone his decision again and again."

Before Isaac left, Barrow had given him some advice. "Remember, the statute about entering Holy Orders may not be enforced now, but the one about marriage is! At no time during the seven-year period of his fellowship may a man marry."

Seven years! Much as he wanted to remain at Cambridge, would that be fair to Catherine?

Once back at work, however, Isaac's downcast spirits disappeared. He plunged eagerly into further study of optics. Day after day he experimented with telescope lenses.

In April he bought a triangular glass prism at a

fair. He wanted to experiment with the rainbow colors the prism made. He also wanted to investigate his new idea in mathematics. Was there ever time enough for everything? he wondered.

To his horror, alarming bulletins arrived from London in the spring of 1665. The plague!

The dread disease, carried by flea-bearing rats, was everywhere in England's capital city. Thousands of people were dying.

Isaac searched through the pages of his old notebook. "Long ago I copied down an ancient recipe for balsam medicine," he explained to Dr. Barrow.

He read the remedy aloud. Barrow shook his head doubtfully.

"I'm going to make some. It's worth a try," Isaac decided. "Apothecary Clark claimed it was good for measles, smallpox, and plague."

As terrified Londoners fled from the city, the plague spread towards Cambridge. Late in June, Isaac packed his telescope, lenses, and the expensive prism. He bought oranges for his family and caught the coach for home. There should be less danger of the Black Death in the country.

By August, Cambridge University was closed.

8. The Year of Miracles

It was summertime in the country. Farmers raked hay, piling up the mounds to turn golden in the sunshine. Sheep grazed near the hedges.

Newton's mother welcomed him happily. "You were wise to come home to Woolsthorpe, Isaac," she said.

"I can help with the farm while I'm here," he offered. "This forced vacation may last several months."

Mrs. Smith recalled broken barn doors and lost sheep. "Oh, no," she told him firmly. "Your brother Benjamin and I manage very well, and your sisters help in the house. You rest and study, Isaac."

Isaac found it pleasant just to sit and think. He was full of ideas. There was the problem with his telescope—somehow he must get a sharper focus. He wanted to experiment with those colors his prism produced too. And his new ideas in mathematics certainly should be developed. He would need them for further study of the heavens.

Scientists everywhere were interested in the movement of planets. As the summer months passed and the university remained closed, Isaac began considering the mystery of celestial mechanics.

What caused the planets to move in orbits around the sun? he asked. And for that matter, what held the moon in its orbit around the earth? This last question had puzzled Isaac Newton since 1664 when he had tracked the comet across the winter skies. Could a single force be responsible both for the movement of the planets and of the moon? he wondered.

"We know a natural force we call gravity which explains the falling of things to earth," Newton mused. "Probably a natural law governs celestial movement as well. When we finally discover it, I believe that law will be one we can express in a simple, mathematical way."

As the plague raged on and vacation days turned into months, Newton was haunted by the problem. Evening after evening he went to a meadow clearing where he could observe the night sky. Dawn found him still staring at the heavens with weary eyes.

Shepherds watched him wander home in time for breakfast. "Poor Mrs. Smith," they said. "Young Newton is good for nothing but the university."

His mother defended him fiercely. "He's thinking," she explained to the family when Isaac sat for hours, scarcely moving.

Newton had studied the works of the great astronomers at Cambridge. Now he reviewed their teachings with the full power of his extraordinary mind. "Their discoveries seem like bits and pieces of a puzzle," he decided. "There is a relationship somewhere, and I intend to find it."

He knew the ancient Greeks believed that the earth hung motionless in the center of the universe. They thought the sun and stars and moon revolved about the earth in perfect circles. Then in 1543 a

Polish monk, Copernicus, claimed that the earth was not the center of the universe after all. It was, instead, part of a great solar system.

Isaac shifted to a new position on the orchard bench where he was enjoying the autumn sunshine. What a shock Copernicus' ideas must have been to the church authorities, he thought. For a time scholars were forbidden to teach his theory of a sun-centered universe in which earth was only one of the planets.

Kepler's work might hold the next clue in this puzzle of celestial motion, Newton decided. The German astronomer's laws of planetary movement, published in 1609, described orbits of the planets as ellipses. Also, Kepler's calculations showed that a planet's speed accelerates as it nears the sun. Somehow that fact seemed important, Isaac thought.

Could Galileo's writings be the next step in solving the puzzle? Isaac asked himself. The Italian astronomer and mathematician had done much in dynamics, the study of how things on earth move.

Newton's mind ranged over Galileo's work— selecting, rejecting, analyzing facts he could use.

Galileo Galilei

Johannes Kepler

Galileo had stated that once something was moving, it would continue to move straight ahead forever until some force slowed it down.

"That's important," Newton murmured, "that, and Galileo's discovery about free-falling objects." The Italian scientist's experiments showed that all things, no matter what their weight, fall to earth at the same speed.

"Isaac! Supper time!" It was the voice of his half-sister.

"Tell mother to go ahead, Mary. There's something I must finish first."

His thoughts plunged back to the problem. Yes, Kepler and his astronomy, then Galileo and his study of motion. Instinctively, Newton knew he was moving in the right direction.

This was the way he liked to work and the way he worked best. First, he analyzed all known facts. Second, he concentrated on the problem for hours at a time. Then, little by little, came the answer to the problem. At times he saw whole solutions in intuitive flashes.

Yes, Newton decided, Galileo's explanation of a body in motion could be used to explain how planets kept moving. There was certainly no friction in space to slow them down. However, Kepler's elliptical orbit was definitely not the straight line that Galileo had described.

"There is another force at work," Newton reasoned, "a force that is powerful enough to pull the moving planets into their closed orbits around the sun."

Something stirred in his memory. When he was a boy playing alone, he had sometimes tied a stone to a heavy string and whirled the stone around and around in great circles. He remembered the tug on the string as the stone tried to escape. If the cord broke, he recalled, the stone went flying off in a straight line.

"H'm, Galileo's straight line," Newton murmured. "The string was the force powerful enough to pull the stone into that circular pattern."

Of course there were no strings in the sky, nothing that the sun could pull on to force the planets into orbit. "And yet there is a force," Newton insisted. "It is invisible, powerful, and unfailing."

An apple falling from the nearby tree hit the ground with a soft thud. Isaac raised his head, thinking fast.

Why had the apple fallen down? The earth force of gravity, everyone knew that—

But why hadn't the apple landed directly below the branch from which it fell? Because of the evening breeze, just gusty enough to blow the apple off its straight-line course to earth—

There was no stopping him now. Newton's imagination moved boldly in giant steps. What if the earth force of gravity, which pulled at the apple, also pulled at the moon? Wouldn't the moon then be falling towards the earth? Yes, but the moon

was very far away and traveling thousands of times faster than the breeze that blew the apple.

Well, what if the force was really a combination of gravity plus the moon's speed and distance? Then the earth's gravity would pull at the moon, but the moon's distance and speed would cause the moon to "fall" past the earth. And wouldn't it fall in a great curve even larger than the earth itself?

Newton jumped to his feet. "A great closed curve —Kepler's elliptical orbit!" he shouted in excitement.

If all this could be true for the moon, why not also for the planets orbiting around the sun? And if the force called gravity here on earth was also an invisible, powerful force in the sky, why, then gravity was everywhere. Was it possible that the law of nature that governed the fall of apples in the orchard also governed the stars above?

"A universal gravitation . . ." Isaac Newton whispered the daring words. "It would mean that all parts of our universe are interrelated."

"Isaac! Robert is here to talk with you." Now Hannah, Isaac's favorite half-sister, had come to fetch him.

"Now why would Robert Barton want to see me?" Isaac teased.

Hannah blushed. "It's about our wedding."

"Well, planning for a marriage is surely more important than holding up the moon," Isaac answered her. Laughing, they ran back to the house.

During the following days Newton searched for ways to test his new hypothesis. How exactly did gravity work? he wondered.

It seemed obvious that its strange pulling force was not equally strong at all distances. Logically, the force of gravity would become weaker as the distance from the earth became greater. But how much weaker?

"These physical relationships must be put into mathematical terms," he reminded himself. "The natural law is bound to be a mathematical law."

At last he had it—the law of inverse square.

"Simple algebra!" Newton beamed. "If gravity obeys this mathematical principle, its force can be calculated to weaken in proportion to the square of the distance between the objects."

At the age of only twenty-four, Newton had hit

upon the fundamentals of a law of nature—the law of universal gravitation. However, he was a scientist. He would not be satisfied until a mathematical proof could be completed.

Newton hurried in to his desk. Using the earth measurements available from Galileo's time, he calculated pages of equations. The results were disappointing. Newton began the problems a second time, watching carefully for errors. Again the calculations did not produce the results he hoped for.

"It answers pretty nearly," he decided. However, that was not good enough for Isaac Newton. Well, he would put it all away for a while and test his ideas again after further thought. He pushed his notes aside and spent the rest of the night in the orchard watching the moon.

"You will make yourself sick," his mother scolded next morning. "Up all night gazing at the stars. Go get some sleep, Isaac."

But a sunny day was perfect for experimenting with his prism. It was amusing to watch colors appear when sunlight struck the triangular glass.

This was nothing new. Hundreds of men before

him had observed these rainbow bands. Isaac stared at the prism in his hand. Why did the colors form? What exactly was light itself?

One textbook stated that white light was simple, and colored light was a complication. Isaac snorted. That said nothing at all. Besides, of all the explanations for color, not one had experiments to prove it was true.

Opening his notebook, Newton wrote: "What is the Nature of Light?"

For his first experiment he simply darkened his room by closing the window shutters, then punched a small hole in one shutter to admit a shaft of sunlight. This sunbeam shone through the prism and produced a strip of rainbow colors on the wall.

This he had expected. But why were the colors stretched out like a ribbon and not round like the hole in the shutter? Carefully, he measured the colored band and wrote down the figures.

Experiment followed experiment. "I must try variations," Newton thought. "I'll use different prisms, larger holes in the shutter, afternoon light, as well as morning light. Yes, even sunlight from different seasons of the year."

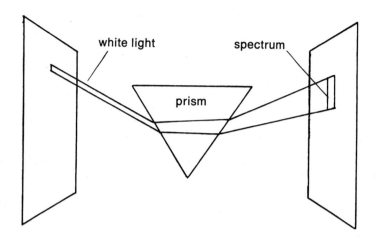

Newton showed that white light passing through a prism bent into colored rays, forming a spectrum.

The colors always appeared in the same order: red, orange, yellow, green, blue, indigo, and violet. The pattern remained oblong in shape.

Each time Newton measured the results and recorded the facts. To the band of colors he gave the Latin name of *spectrum*.

After many days of experimentation, he felt certain of one fact: White light passing through a prism bent into separate colored rays, which spread out to form the spectrum on his bedroom wall.

"White light is a mixture of these colored rays,"

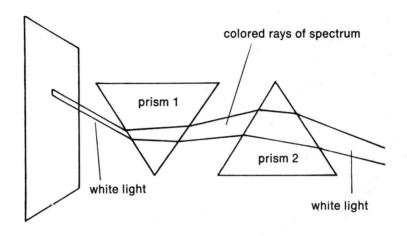

The colored rays of the spectrum passing through a
second inverted prism turned into white light.

Newton noted. "The prism merely reveals to the
eye what is there in white light all the time."

Could he prove it?

Working alone in the small room at Woolsthorpe,
Isaac Newton thought of an experiment to test his
theory. First he used a glass prism to separate a
ray of sunlight into the familiar spectrum, which
was thrown on the wall opposite the window. Next
he placed a second prism of the same size directly
in the path of light coming through the first prism.
He turned the second prism until all the colors

This old print shows Isaac Newton performing his
first experiment demonstrating that white light is
composed of colored rays of light.

overlapped, recombining again into the white light.

Triumphantly, Newton seized his pen and began to write. He had demonstrated that white light was indeed a mixture of all the colors of the spectrum.

Excited with his discovery, Isaac tried another experiment. First he passed a ray of white light through a prism, forming a spectrum. Next he cut a small slot in a board. He planned to pass each colored ray through the slot, one at a time. First the violet ray was slipped through the slot and passed through a second prism. The violet ray emerged still violet. The orange ray emerged orange.

The results were the same for each pure colored beam. He could not change its color.

Newton called this experiment his "crucial test." His alert mind recognized it as proof that pure colored rays were not mixtures. He had demonstrated that only white light, a mixture of all the colors, produced the spectrum.

Moreover, he had discovered a curious thing: Each color of the spectrum was refracted or bent at a different angle by the prism. Violet was refracted the most, red the least.

"This unequal refraction causes both the shape of the spectrum and its unchanging color pattern," Newton concluded.

While Cambridge University remained closed, Newton pursued the secrets of light and color. His investigations took him further in this field than any man before.

It was a time when most scientists still believed that the best way to gain knowledge was by meeting together to debate ideas. Isaac Newton, however, carried out careful experiments and recorded observations. His journals grew thick with notes, sketches, and equations.

This devotion to his work made Catherine unhappy. "You haven't visited me in weeks," she complained. "I came to see if you were ill."

Isaac looked at her solemn face. "I'm sorry I worried you, Catherine. I get so caught up—"

"I know," she interrupted with a faint smile. "You get so caught up with your ideas that you forget me."

"We must remedy that," Isaac assured her. a picnic this afternoon."

morning, however, Isaac was back at

work. "Now I will test my new mathematical method," he decided, "the one I was working on just before I left Cambridge."

To prove to himself that his original system of mathematics would work, Newton walked to the village of Boothby. There he used his new system of mathematics to measure the square footage framed by the arches of an old manor house. As each arch curved, its distance from the ground changed. He eagerly carried out his answer to fifty-two decimal places.

Newton saw the usefulness of his method of calculation for dealing with problems that measured change. Today the method is named calculus, but Newton called it "fluxions," from the Latin word for flowing or changing.

It was indeed a mathematics of change—changing direction, changing velocity, changing time, changing position, changing size, and even the rates of change in these changing variables themselves!

"This is the mathematical tool I need for further work on the movement of heavenly bodies," Newton realized. During the quiet weeks at

Woolsthorpe he spent many long days developing fluxions.

Late in March 1667, news came that Cambridge University was reopening.

"My long vacation is over," Isaac told his family. He gathered together the notebooks holding the light experiments, his work on gravitation, and the problems solved with fluxions.

In less than a year and a half, his penetrating mind and intuitive skill had laid the scientific groundwork for the advances of generations of scientists to come. Any one of his three major achievements would have gained him immortal fame, and all three great discoveries were made in Newton's twenty-third and twenty-fourth years. From that time forward, everything Isaac Newton accomplished was a development or an improvement of his Woolsthorpe projects.

Isaac remembered it this way: "I was in the prime of my age for invention, and minded mathematics and philosophy [science] more than at any time since."

Historians would speak of these golden months at Woolsthorpe as Newton's year of miracles.

9. First Fame

The April skies were overcast, but Isaac felt cheerful. He sloshed through the rain puddles in Trinity's courtyard to Dr. Barrow's quarters.

"Well, Newton," the professor greeted him. "I spent the time away from Cambridge in religious work. What did you do?"

Isaac hesitated. Should he tell his tutor about the Woolsthorpe projects involving white light and gravitation? No, he decided. Without full proof it was too soon to speak of discoveries.

"I worked on that mathematical idea I told you about before the plague," he admitted shyly. "And I thought about new shapes for telescope lenses."

Within a week it seemed to Isaac as if he had

never been away from Cambridge. The excitement of science crowded out everything else.

He spent many evenings with Dr. Barrow, discussing optics. Each night he sat up late, writing in his notebook by candlelight.

Early in December of 1667 the college authorities announced their decision. The promising scholar from Lincolnshire would be elected to fill a fellowship vacancy, they said.

That night Isaac sat by the window watching snowflakes fall. His heart was full of a great private joy.

"I'll spend Christmas at Woolsthorpe," he decided. He was eager to share this news with his mother. Isaac knew that he must also tell Catherine that she should wait no longer for him.

Catherine herself made his errand easier. "Why, I'd be an old maid if I waited for you to finish being a scholar, Isaac Newton. And me with a dozen lads just begging me to say the word!"

"Now you're teasing me," he protested.

Catherine touched his hand gently. "I think I've known for a year that it would be this way," she said. "Don't worry about me, Isaac."

Isaac smiled. Bless her! "We'll always be good friends, Catherine," he promised.

In a way, Isaac Newton thought, that talk with Catherine marked the end of the old life. A few months later he completed his Master of Arts degree and became a Major Fellow of Trinity College.

Now that he was a member of the college staff, Newton received a small salary, his dinners, and free fellowship lodgings. The quarters assigned to him were in Great Court, next to Trinity's Great Gate, and included a small enclosed garden.

Isaac overflowed with plans. He would attack his Woolsthorpe projects again; he would assist Dr. Barrow in preparing his optics manuscripts for the printer; he would fix up a chemistry laboratory in the little hut in his garden.

"First of all, I'm going to London to buy glassware for my optical studies and chemical equipment for investigating metals in my laboratory," he told Barrow. "I want to build a better telescope."

Barrow was interested. "Will you have the London glassworkers grind your lenses?"

"No, indeed," Isaac protested. "I want to do everything with my own hands."

Soon the noise of hammering sounded from Newton's garden. Astonished Fellows watched him construct a small laboratory furnace inside the garden hut.

"The new science of chemistry puzzles them," Isaac told his former roommate Wickins, who had come to watch him while he worked. "Also," he grinned, "they've never seen a Cambridge Fellow lay bricks before."

At least Wickins and Barrow understand me, Isaac thought gratefully. They never disturbed him if they found him staring off into space, concentrating on a problem.

One problem bothered him for a long time.

"I've experimented for weeks with my lenses," Newton explained to Professor Barrow. The two were talking in Isaac's laboratory one day after it was finished. "It's impossible to get a satisfactory focus with the kind of telescope we now use."

The trouble was that refracting telescopes could not bring stars into sharp focus. The image always blurred with a fringe of colors.

From his experiments with prisms, Isaac knew what must be wrong. The telescope lens was simply behaving like a prism, bending the light passing through it into colored rays.

"We're still using telescopes like the ones Galileo made sixty years ago," Newton objected. "I propose to build a telescope that uses a curved mirror rather than a lens. It's an idea suggested by the Scottish mathematician James Gregory. He lacked the mechanical skill to construct one, however."

While they talked, Isaac moved contentedly about the laboratory. He stirred the liquid bubbling in a glass beaker. Carefully, he added charcoal to the fire under a clay crucible.

Barrow's eyes studied the equipment on the shelves: flasks and retorts, stone jars full of acids, the strange distilling apparatus called an alembic, even a water bath.

Isaac noted the interest. "I'll be constructing the entire telescope right here," he said.

During most of 1668 Newton worked to build the first reflecting telescope. The mirror was made of a metal he prepared himself. Copper, arsenic, and tin were heated together until they melted, forming an alloy that hardened white as silver. When the silvery disc cooled, Isaac ground it to a concave surface shaped like a shallow saucer. Polishing took great patience. At last a tiny reflector mirror only one inch in diameter was ready.

The completed telescope was a metal tube just six inches long, but it magnified forty times.

"Why, that is as powerful as a lens telescope six feet long!" Barrow exclaimed. "Tell me how it works."

"The little mirror rests at the bottom of the metal tube, reflecting light back up the tube itself. This light is then reflected sideways by a smaller flat mirror set at an angle inside of the tube."

Newton paused. "See the eyepiece set in the side of the telescope? That part is my invention. Look through this lens eyepiece. The reflected light can be easily focused and observed. Here, try it yourself."

The professor turned the little instrument starward. Jupiter's shining image flashed into his view. "It's a perfect focus!" he cried out. "You have solved the problem of the color fringe, Newton."

Today, 300 years later, the side eyepiece arrangement is still used in reflecting telescopes. It is called the *Newtonian focus.*

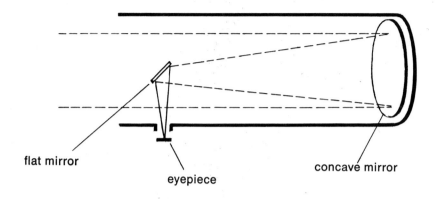

flat mirror

eyepiece

concave mirror

This diagram of Newton's telescope shows how the
light is reflected by mirrors to the eyepiece.

One evening soon after this, Dr. Barrow climbed
the outside staircase leading to Newton's quarters.
He pushed past the students and professors crowd-
ing around the telescope at the top of the steps.
Barrow pounded on his friend's door.

"Read this, Mr. Newton," the professor said,
handing a paper to Isaac. "Nicolaus Mercator, the
German mathematician living in London, sug-
gests a way to compute the area bounded by a
curve. This has never been done, and his idea may
not work. Somehow, his calculations remind me of
what you were doing before the plague."

"It is almost the same," Newton agreed after

examining the paper. "However, I know my method works, Barrow. I used it to measure the area under a hyperbola."

"You have actually tested your method, Newton?"

"Indeed, yes. I measured some arches near my home and carried out the calculation to fifty-two decimal places."

"Will you prepare a paper explaining your method?" asked the professor. "I want to share your work with my colleagues at the Royal Society of London." Isaac knew that this important group of men had been organized to promote scientific knowledge. They would no doubt be interested. "And John Collins, he should surely see the paper too," Barrow added.

Isaac asked, "John Collins?"

"Collins is a mathematician who acts as a sort of clearinghouse for new scientific ideas," Barrow explained. "He writes letters to interested people telling them about advances in various fields."

"Oh." Newton's voice was uncertain.

Barrow clapped the younger man on the back. "You know, with books so expensive and so few scientific journals, there's really no better way to share your ideas with the scientific community. This may make you famous. You'll allow Collins to circulate written copies among European mathematicians, won't you?"

Newton agreed, but reluctantly. He worked mainly for his own satisfaction, and being famous was the last thing the shy scholar wanted.

His paper "On Analysis of Equations with an Infinite Number of Terms" was published in 1669. Soon excited scientists everywhere were discussing it. Even Newton was pleased when Leibniz, the great German mathematician, wrote him asking for further information.

Word soon came from London that the Royal Society was deeply interested in both Newton's telescope, of which they had been informed, and the mathematical paper with the long title. Barrow was delighted. He had been hoping to leave the university for a while and devote himself to religious work as chaplain for King Charles. Now that Newton's brilliance was recognized, the problem of finding a suitable replacement for the Lucasian Professorship seemed solved.

"I am recommending you to follow me as professor of mathematics," he told Newton.

Newton could scarely believe his good fortune. The duties were light: one lecture a week during winter term, plus student conferences. There would be money now for whatever scientific work he wished to do.

On October 29, 1669, 26-year-old Isaac Newton became Lucasian Professor in the university he had entered eight years before as a humble sizar. Catherine, happily married now, and his mother proudly spread the news to all of Lincolnshire.

Isaac wished he shared their confidence. What if words failed him when he appeared in the lecture hall? Nervously, he prepared his first talk.

The hall was filled with students and Fellows. Had everyone come to hear? Newton worried. Shyly, he read his latest research on the spectrum. As the last Latin word was spoken, faculty members moved forward with congratulations.

Bewildered students shook their heads. The man was a genius, but they didn't understand a word he had said! One by one they hurried away to the library.

10. White Light and New Rivals

Newton gave the new telescope one last polishing. Then he carefully mounted it on a metal ball fitted into a socket in a heavy piece of wood.

There! Now the little instrument could be swiveled in any direction.

Newton wrapped the telescope in soft cloths and packed it carefully for the journey to London.

"Remember," he instructed the waiting messenger, "deliver everything to Dr. Barrow at Whitehall." He watched the youth stride off. If winter rains did not delay the coach, Barrow should have the telescope in London within two days.

Isaac Newton sighed. Perhaps now he could get back to his own lectures and research again. The

Royal Society's request for a telescope for King Charles II had arrived at an inconvenient time.

Well, His Majesty would soon have the instrument, Isaac grumbled. All this fuss over his little telescope!

No one but Newton was surprised when exciting news came from London some weeks later. Newton, the announcement declared, had been elected to

Newton's original reflecting telescope. Notice the eyepiece set in the side of the tube.

membership in the Royal Society on January 11, 1672.

"The king must really have liked that telescope," Isaac said wonderingly.

John Wickins laughed. "I'd say it means that the Society recognizes you as a scientist of great merit."

The two friends sat alone at last in Isaac's rooms near Great Gate. Newton marveled at the number of professors who had climbed his staircase that day to offer congratulations.

Wickins looked thoughtfully at Isaac. People said the young professor lived only for his experiments, forgetting everything else while his mind focused on a new idea. Now famous scientists praised his telescope. Would all this change his friend?

"I suppose you'll go to London for the Royal Society meetings?" he asked.

Newton shrugged. "They meet every Wednesday. It's too long a trip to make regularly. I'd get nothing else done."

"You work too hard," Wickins cautioned him. "You're only thirty, yet your hair is gray."

"It isn't study that turned it gray," Newton joked. "I've been experimenting with quicksilver. Work with mercury, John, and your hair too quick turns silver!"

Wickins left, smiling at the witty remark.

Newton sat alone by the fire, considering the honor that had come to him. He would enjoy knowing the Society's distinguished members, he thought with pride.

There was brilliant Robert Hooke—scientist, inventor, and the Society's official experimenter. Hooke was interested in microscopes, plant life, gravity, and fossils. In fact, Newton decided, Hooke was interested in almost everything.

Christopher Wren, professor of astronomy at Oxford University, was better known as the architect who was rebuilding London's St. Paul's Cathedral after the Great Fire of 1666. Wren was a popular leader in the Society, Newton knew.

There were John Locke, the physician–philosopher, and Samuel Pepys of the Royal Navy, a man whose interest in science went back almost to the beginning of the Society itself. Then there was the mathematician John Collins with whom he had already corresponded; his friend Barrow was a member, and there were many others.

However, the man he wanted most to know was Robert Boyle.

Boyle had helped to found the Royal Society. He was an unusually skilled scientist, a chemist who would one day be known as the "father of modern chemistry."

Newton had heard that the wealthy Boyle conducted experiments in a splendidly equipped private laboratory. There he studied the combining of metals.

How similar our interests are, Newton thought. He resolved to write to Boyle about the new science they both loved—chemistry.

As a matter of fact, Newton decided, why not share some of his discoveries with all these new friends? The Society members would probably find his work with the spectrum even more interesting than the telescope.

With great care he prepared a paper, "The Composition of White Light." It was a full account of the optics experiments.

Newton arranged his observations in good order, using clear phrases to describe his methods. Mathematical measurements were exactly reported. In closing, he stated the results of the experiments. He explained what those measured results proved about white light and colored light.

"I'm sending the report to the secretary to be read before the membership," Isaac told Wickins. "I really prefer to wait here for their reactions. I'll work in my laboratory and also begin some research of Bible history."

Isaac Newton performed experiments in this crude laboratory in his rooms at Trinity College.

At first the paper "met with great applause." The Royal Society ordered "that the author be solemnly thanked. . ." Arrangements were made to print Newton's paper in the Society's records and to circulate copies to scientists in Europe. Finally, a committee under Hooke's direction was appointed to study the report more fully.

Robert Hooke sat quietly through the meeting. Hooke was badly crippled, and constant pain made him irritable. He had a jealous nature, and the members' enthusiasm for Newton irked him. He refused to accept Newton's theory of white light because it clashed with his own explanation.

Practically ignoring his committee, Hooke prepared the official reply for the new member waiting at Cambridge.

The dispatch stunned Newton. The committee questioned his experimental methods and his findings.

"Colors are created by the prism, not revealed by it," Hooke insisted. "White light is pure." Newton's experiments were not original at all, he went on to say. They included much mathematical nonsense.

Established scientists everywhere joined the argument. This stung Newton's sensitive pride, although his friends reminded him that such debate was usual.

"Pioneers of new ideas must expect critical discussion," they warned.

"Discussion and debate prove nothing," Newton told John Wickins. "My work is based on factual evidence from carefully controlled experiments. Why don't members of the Royal Society and the other scientists simply repeat my experiments and reproduce the results themselves?"

At first Newton answered every critic with a polite letter, defending his experimental procedures. He wrote:

> The best and safest method seems to be first to inquire diligently into the properties of things ... establishing these properties by experiments, and then to proceed more slowly to the explanation of them ...

Only a fool could believe that the truths of science are discovered by arguing about them, he thought bitterly.

The public quarrel dragged on for three years. The final blows came from Hooke. Newton's powerful rival announced that he himself had made a reflecting telescope some four years before the Cambridge fledgling. What caused Newton even greater pain was Hooke's sly hint that Newton stole ideas from other men.

"I have wasted my precious time in useless letters and discussions with fools," Newton cried out in disgust.

The report that Newton had sent the Society would one day be recognized as a classic contribution to science. It was the first completely experimental investigation of light and color. In 1672, however, it represented nothing but trouble to Isaac Newton.

"It was a mistake to share my discoveries with the scientific brotherhood. Never again!" swore Newton. In the future his ideas would belong only to himself and the few students who understood his lectures.

All Isaac Newton wanted now was the peace of former days and the privacy of his own laboratory at Cambridge.

11. A Petition to the King

At the first light of day, Isaac liked to be up and walking in his garden. He paced the narrow paths, enjoying the fresh air and the morning quiet.

Suddenly a new idea set his mind whirling.

He turned abruptly and rushed up the staircase leading to his rooms. Standing at the study table, he wrote carefully in his notebook.

True to his promise, Newton had turned his back on the Royal Society that dared to criticize him and was deep in his own research again. In the months that followed, he reviewed old manuscripts telling the history of Christianity. He devoted weeks at a time to chemistry experiments.

Like Boyle, he melted metals, recombining them into strange new alloys.

Cambridge undergraduates saw Newton as an absentminded professor. "Sometimes he forgets to dine," they chuckled.

"What you call absentmindedness is a sign of Newton's power of concentration," his friend Barrow explained. "The professor's thoughts are occupied with science."

Dr. Barrow had returned to Cambridge in 1673 when King Charles appointed him Master of Trinity. Under Barrow's supervision, old rules from the royal statutes were being enforced. The new Master hoped these changes would restore Trinity to former greatness.

"Unfortunately, one of these rules affects you," he told Newton. "A Trinity fellowship is for seven years, you know. During that time a Fellow is expected to complete his religious studies and be ordained a minister. After that, he may apply for a renewed fellowship and remain at Trinity as a teaching-clergyman."

Newton nodded. He knew the old rule, but it had not been enforced for many years.

Newton (left) spent his most productive years as a scientist at Trinity. In a letter (below) to the Royal Society in London, he describes one of his experiments.

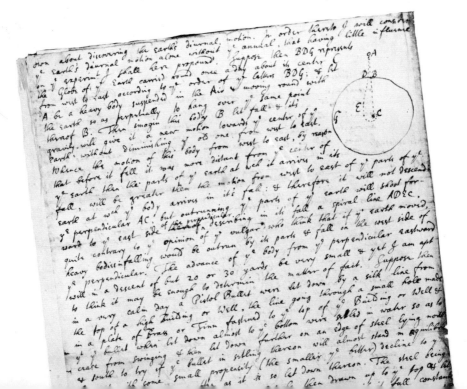

"My seven years are nearly over," he said. "To renew my fellowship must I enter Holy Orders?"

Dr. Barrow sighed. "Yes, according to Trinity's charter rules."

"Each man serves God in his own way," Newton said after a thoughtful silence. "My way is through science, not by entering the ministry. Tell me, will this mean I lose the Lucasian Professorship also?"

Barrow made a quick decision. "Both Trinity College and England need your dedicated mind," he said. "Let's appeal directly to the Crown. We will petition His Majesty to grant an exception to the royal statutes in your case."

Newton flinched. To beg favors at Court was humiliating.

"It's worth a try," Barrow said gently. "Remember how enthusiastically King Charles received your telescope?"

Early in February 1675, Newton traveled to London. He dreaded the visit and worried about the work he left behind him. However, the city was full of pleasant surprises. Important people visited his lodgings, offering assistance for his mission. Scientists pledged him their public support.

All this pleased Isaac Newton. He presented his petition at Court and nervously sat back to wait.

"I could visit Robert Boyle," he decided. They had corresponded for years.

The fifty-year-old scientist welcomed Newton to his house in Pall Mall. The two men spent hours in Boyle's laboratory, discussing chemistry.

"Since my illness, I go out seldom," Boyle admitted. "However, I want to attend next Wednesday's Royal Society meeting with you."

On February 18, Henry Oldenburg, secretary of the Royal Society, proudly introduced Newton to the membership.

"This is my first formal meeting," Newton acknowledged. "I am delighted that experiments will be performed today." He looked with interest at the tables of equipment.

When Sir Christopher Wren came forward to meet him, Newton bowed. "Barrow sends you greetings," Isaac said.

"Sit with me and my friends," Wren invited. "I have waited months to make your acquaintance, Newton."

Isaac enjoyed the meeting. The members' praise

of his work pleased him. Even Robert Hooke received him with friendly courtesy.

"Next week we plan to repeat your prism experiments," Hooke said.

"If I am still in London, I'll come," Newton promised.

"You'll be here," everyone assured him. "Petitions at Court drag on for months."

As the days passed, Isaac Newton could only agree. It was disappointing, too, when Hooke kept canceling the prism experiments.

Finally on March 12 a message from the king arrived at Newton's lodgings. King Charles was pleased to grant the petition, Isaac read. To show the high regard in which England held the Cambridge scientist, Newton would be allowed to keep his Trinity fellowship without taking Holy Orders, for so long as he remained Lucasian Professor.

Newton said good-bye to his new friends. His mind at peace again, he returned eagerly to his unfinished experiments.

On December 9, 1675, the Royal Society received Newton's second paper on further experiments with light.

Hooke exploded. Hadn't he announced earlier that light, like sound, consisted of waves? Now here was Newton stating that light probably was a stream of small, swiftly moving particles. Newton said that these particles, or corpuscles, traveled in uneven surges of motion.

"What is this nonsense of a corpuscular theory?" the older scientist questioned publicly. He chose to ignore the important other half of Newton's idea, the part about wavelike, uneven surges. That idea was similar to Hooke's own.

Newton was angered by Hooke's attack on his new work in optics. "If my discoveries are ever published again, it will be after my death," he vowed.

In the years that followed, scientists first favored Newton's corpuscular theory of light. Then, during the nineteenth century, the wave theory associated with Hooke became the accepted explanation. Not until Einstein and other great physicists of the twentieth century published their findings did scientists conclude that light indeed possessed dual characteristics much like the ones Newton had suggested back in 1675.

12. On the Shoulders of Giants

It was an August afternoon in 1684. Isaac Newton stood at his laboratory table, rereading Robert Boyle's letter. From time to time he peered at the powdered metal heating in the clay container on the furnace grill. The strong odor from sulfuric acid filled the room.

Newton mopped his sweaty face with a corner of his academic gown. "The metal is not dissolving properly," he muttered. "Perhaps my furnace fire is not as hot as Boyle's."

"Mr. Newton?"

The 41-year-old scientist looked up with a frown. In his laboratory doorway stood a friendly faced young stranger.

"I'm Edmond Halley from London. Sir Christopher Wren thought you might help me."

Newton eyed his uninvited visitor. Although he and the famous architect stayed in touch by letters, Wren had never sent anyone to see him before.

Halley . . . the name echoed in Isaac's memory. Of course—Halley was the astronomer who had traveled to the Mediterranean Sea to study southern stars.

"I've read about your star catalog in the records of the Royal Society," Newton acknowledged. "Very informative. But why are you here?"

Halley came straight to the point. "I'm interested in planetary orbits, and I need your help with a problem. What would be the shape of a planet's path around the sun, if gravity weakens according to the square of the distance between that planet and the sun?"

"An ellipse," Newton answered firmly.

"How do you know, sir?"

"I've proved it mathematically." Newton was pleased at his guest's delight. "Perhaps I can find my calculations for you."

They searched through the jumble of notes scattered everywhere over desk and table. "I threw them in some drawer," Newton insisted. "Let me see, it was about five years ago—"

Halley gasped. "Professor, many of us in the Royal Society are working on the mysteries of planetary orbits. Some of us have even guessed that the force between two heavenly bodies decreases with increasing distance, probably according to the inverse-square law. However, we have not found the proof. Have you known this great truth for five years and told nobody?"

Newton smiled. "Five years? No, it's more like twenty years. I deduced an inverse-square relationship in determining my law of gravitation back in 1666 at Woolsthorpe. However, I lacked certain data to make my mathematical proof accurate, so I put the work aside."

He paused, remembering. "Then five years ago some incident set me pondering on the planets again. By that time accurate earth measurements were available and I was able to complete my proof. The entire mystery of planetary movement dissolved into a simple mathematical explanation."

"Mr. Newton, we must locate those calculations," Halley insisted.

The dedicated Cambridge scientist felt drawn to this enthusiastic young man. "It will be no great trouble to rework the problems," he assured his visitor. "I'll send them to you in London."

In November 1684, Halley received the promised calculations. Precious equations and explanations were scribbled on odds and ends of paper.

Halley examined the material and knew it to be the earth-shaking information. Here were answers to the mystery of the falling moon and the reasons for the elliptical paths of the planets! Hastily he made plans to return to Trinity College.

Isaac Newton greeted his London visitor warmly. "What brings you again to Cambridge?" he inquired.

"I've come to urge you to publish your discoveries. Do you realize the importance of your astounding theory of gravity?" Halley asked. "While you keep silent, others are catching up. Hooke, for example, is developing ideas along similar lines."

Newton shook his head. "Nine years ago I was

willing to publish my work. What a distressing time I had! I vowed then to publish nothing more in my lifetime."

Halley frowned. "What a waste—"

Isaac Newton paced back and forth. "My life is good as it is, Mr. Halley," he interrupted. "I have developed my theories on forces and motion. I have explored more of the science of optics. All this I share with my students. There is a small band of brilliant students here—young men like Charles Montagu. They're forming a science society, and I meet with them."

He selected some papers from the clutter on his desk. "These may interest you—my lecture notes since last October. As you will see, this term I devoted my lectures to considering how things move. 'The Motion of Bodies' is the title I gave to the series."

Halley studied the papers with rising excitement. Here were explanations of a mystery that had baffled astronomers for ages.

"Mr. Newton," he said, "the value of all this cannot be measured. In this curious work you have moved from solution and mathematical proof of the original problem to important generalizations. I plead with you, sir, to publish this manuscript."

Newton was appalled. "And lose the peace and privacy I need for thinking?"

Edmond Halley struck back with a final argument. "Communication is slow, but word of your work drifts up to London. Let me register this set of lectures with the Royal Society. That will establish the priority of your discovery for England," he prodded. "Otherwise every scientist in Europe will seize upon your ideas and develop them, each for his own advancement."

The color drained from Isaac Newton's face.

Now Halley spoke more gently. "I am a mathematician and astronomer of some reputation, Mr. Newton. I will put my work aside to assist you if you publish. Your discoveries will revolutionize scientific thinking. It would be an honor to play even a small part in presenting them to mankind."

Moved by the younger man's sincere enthusiasm, Newton yielded.

Halley hurried back to London with the manuscript of lectures to present to the Royal Society.

The astronomer was triumphant. He also had Newton's promise to begin writing a full account of his discoveries in physics and mathematics.

Halley was certain that the Royal Society would be eager to publish such a book. "I will take care of the details of producing the book and will shield you from publicity," he promised the professor.

Newton set to work. At first he planned only a small volume, an expansion of his recent Cambridge lectures on how things move. But never in his life had Newton been content to do anything halfway. As he wrote, new ideas overflowed the pages, and a great book began to form.

Isaac Newton's years of creative thinking and scientific research were recorded in journals and notebooks, scribbled on scraps of paper, and scattered everywhere. Now he planned to structure all the parts and pieces into one great mathematical explanation of the system of the world.

Of course it would be written in Latin, the language of scholars. Newton had the title in mind as well: *Philosophiae Naturalis Principia Mathematica*—"Mathematical Principles of Natural Philosophy."

As Newton settled down to write, it gradually became apparent that the work divided naturally into three parts, which Newton called "books."

At times his mind reeled with the immensity of the task before him. During the eighteen months following Halley's visit he worked relentlessly day and night on the bold undertaking. His own characteristic stick-to-itiveness and Halley's encouraging letters and visits kept him from giving up. For relaxation in between writing, Newton worked in his chemistry laboratory.

The book became Newton's whole life. "He forgets to eat his meals," old Deborah, the college maid, complained. "I bring food on a tray to his chamber, but in the morning I carry it away, scarcely tasted."

A secretary, young Humphrey Newton, was hired to copy the scientist's pages into neat, handwritten Latin for the printer. (Although the young man had the same last name as his new employer, he was not related to him.) Humphrey worked hard to keep up with Newton, for the scientist hardly even stopped to eat or sleep. Often Newton sat on the edge of his bed for hours, lost in thought.

The printing of the *Principia* was authorized at a meeting of the Royal Society in London.

Day after day the tremendous effort continued. Then one spring morning the manuscript was finished.

With embarrassment, the Royal Society now discovered that it could find no money in its treasury to publish the great effort. In this new emergency, Edmond Halley offered to pay all printing costs. The June 2, 1686 minutes of the Society recorded that he was given permission to do so.

The *Principia* is often called the greatest creative

work produced by one man. Many people consider it the most important scientific book ever written.

Book I of the *Principia* is concerned with the motion of the bodies in free space. Within this important first portion are Newton's famous three laws of motion:

> First Law—*A body at rest will remain at rest and a body in motion will remain in motion at the same speed and in the same direction unless acted upon by an outside force.*

This first law explains why, when an automobile which is traveling at fifty miles an hour unexpectedly stops, the occupant shoots forward at fifty miles an hour unless the "outside force" of a fastened seat belt acts upon the "body in motion."

> Second Law—*Any change in motion is proportional to the force causing the change and takes place in the straight-line direction of the acting force.*

For example, a greater amount of force is needed to accelerate a race car from the starting line to

100 miles per hour in 10 seconds than is needed to bring it from the starting line to 50 miles per hour in the same amount of time.

Third Law—*For every action there is an equal and opposite reaction.*

Every rocket, from the Fourth-of-July variety to the Saturn rocket launching the Apollo 11 crew on its historic moon-landing flight, obeys Newton's third law of motion.

A more down-to-earth example would be to release a toy balloon filled with air. The air rushes out in one direction from the open neck, pushing the balloon in the opposite direction.

In Book II of the *Principia*, Newton described motion in a resisting medium, such as air or water, and the motion of fluids themselves. He showed methods for measuring the speed of sound and even offered suggestions for streamlining ships. Here, too, are the important experiments with pendulums.

Book III of the *Principia* was called "The System of the World." In it Newton explained that his law of gravitation was *universal* because it

PHILOSOPHIÆ
NATURALIS
PRINCIPIA
MATHEMATICA.

Autore *JS. NEWTON*, *Trin. Coll. Cantab. Soc.* Matheseos
Professore *Lucasiano*, & Societatis Regalis Sodali.

IMPRIMATUR·
S. PEPYS, *Reg. Soc.* PRÆSES.
Julii 5. 1686:

LONDINI,
Jussu Societatis Regiæ ac Typis *Josephi Streater.* Prostant Vena-
les apud *Sam. Smith* ad insignia Principis *Walliæ* in Cœmiterio
D. *Pauli*, aliosq; nonnullos Bibliopolas. *Anno* MDCLXXXVII.

Title page of Newton's *Principia*, first edition

applied to every particle of matter throughout the universe—in the heavens and on earth. He calculated the mass of the sun, the earth, and the moon. He described how comets move. Then, using the law of universal gravitation, he presented a mathematical explanation of ocean tides.

The *Principia* was the masterwork of a master-mind. However, Newton did not forget that there had been great discoverers before him— Archimedes, Copernicus, Tycho Brahe, Kepler, Galileo, Descartes, and others.

"If I have seen further," Isaac Newton said, "it is by standing on the shoulders of giants."

13. Troubled Times

Newton clenched his fists. How dare Hooke claim to be the discoverer of the inverse-square law as it applied to universal gravitation!

"So he accuses me before the Royal Society of stealing his ideas?" Newton said bitterly. "The idea was mine long before Hooke ever spoke of it, and I applied the law itself some twenty years ago in my Woolsthorpe work."

Halley had come from London to soften the bad news. "It is vexing," he agreed, "but few men believe Hooke's charge. Your reputation is safe, Newton. The lectures I registered for you before the Royal Society hold your mathematical proof of universal gravitation."

"Hooke is a jealous mischief-maker." Newton's voice was sharp.

"Could you perhaps mention his name in the preface of the *Principia*?" Halley asked. "After all, Hooke does not pretend the entire law of universal gravitation is his."

"That at least he cannot claim," Newton blazed. "Many scientists have independently thought of a force pulling each planet toward the sun. Indeed, you and I discussed how some were even speculating that the force might vary inversely with the square of the distance. Wren and Huygens—and you, too, Halley—guessed that it was true."

"Thinking it true and proving it true are quite different things," Halley remarked tactfully. "Only you had the insight and knowledge to find the mathematical proof of universal gravitation."

Newton paced back and forth. "This is the fourth time Hooke has jealously attacked my work. I refuse to print the remainder of the *Principia*."

Halley was horrified. Not only was he heavily in debt with publication costs of the *Principia*, but the third part of it was important to him in his own study of comets.

It took days of skillful argument and several diplomatic letters before Halley calmed the angry genius. Then, with dry humor, Newton prepared a single sentence to be added to the book. He briefly acknowledged that Hooke, among others, had shown interest in the mathematical possibility of the inverse-square law as applied to the problem of gravitation. Hooke's name was neatly sandwiched between those of Sir Christopher Wren and Dr. Edmond Halley.

Hard-working Halley grinned—one more crisis over!

Two months later, in July 1687, the most important scientific work ever written by one man was finally published. Samuel Pepys, as president of the Royal Society, signed the order to print the book.

Scientists everywhere hailed the *Principia* as a great achievement. Although they acknowledged the book's importance, few of them understood its difficult mathematics. In time, however, the *Principia* would be recognized as the cornerstone of all future mathematical physics.

Newton's friend Halley was the first astronomer

to use information from the great book. The *Principia* stated that comets, like planets, obeyed the law of universal gravitation. Newton theorized that comets traveled in large elliptical orbits that took years to complete.

"Comets too? The mysterious 'lawless comets'?" Halley puzzled. Perhaps the great comet of 1682 could be used as proof!

Halley searched through ancient records. Descriptions of a similar comet could be found at seventy-five-year intervals.

"It must be the same comet," Halley confided to Newton. "The full proof, however, lies in the future. I predict the 'return' of this comet sometime in 1758, and at approximately seventy-five-year intervals thereafter."

Halley's conclusion was accurate. Watchers of the sky saw the beautiful sight cross the heavens during the winter of 1758–1759. The comet appeared in 1835 and once more in 1910. According to Edmond Halley's timetable, *Halley's Comet* will blaze again into view in 1986.

Also within the pages of the *Principia* were the laws that formed man's stepping stones into space.

Today, space vehicles rocket into orbit at exactly the right speed, right height, and right direction in maneuvers determined by calculations based on Newton's formulas. A stunning proof of Newton's theory of universal gravitation came on July 20, 1969, when the Apollo 11 astronauts, first men to set foot on the moon, landed there safely at a predicted spot and time.

In 1687, the man responsible for it all was looking around for a new challenge.

Newton had enjoyed helping to defend the university in a court case some months earlier, and he decided to ask for another such assignment.

Officials of the university had been impressed by the scientist's firmness in court. Newton himself realized that much of his earlier shyness had left him. Perhaps it is age, he thought, or perhaps success. Anyhow, he was no longer afraid to go out into the world. Indeed, he felt eager for new experiences.

In 1689 the opportunity arrived. The members of Cambridge University elected Newton to represent them in Parliament.

Voices buzzed as the famous Newton was seated

in the House of Commons. Heads turned to see the well-dressed, dignified man with the steady, honest gaze.

Newton was greeted by his former student Charles Montagu, now a member of the House. Later they joined other members of Parliament at a table in a busy London coffeehouse. While aproned waiters served bowls of steaming coffee, Montagu signaled for pipes and tobacco.

"I plan to take little part in the political debates," Newton told Montagu, the powerful young leader of the liberal Whig party. "I intend to be active behind the scenes. My responsibility is to protect the university's interests."

The scientist waved away a second bowl of coffee. "No more, thank you, Charles. I'm meeting John Locke and Lord Monmouth for supper. It's important to get to know the thinking of other members of Parliament. And since Locke is also a member of the Royal Society, I'm hopeful we'll have many common goals."

Montagu whistled softly. There were few signs of the retiring professor in this confident man beside him. "And I worried that a mathematical

Newton enjoyed meeting his London friends at pleasant coffee houses like the one shown above.

hermit would be unhappy among us politicians!" Montagu laughed.

London was full of important people eager to entertain the author of the *Principia*. Newton enjoyed their praise and admiration. After years of study, the excitement of the city pleased him. There were dinners and parties and long conversations with scientific friends.

And always there was the satisfaction of an honest job well done in Parliament.

Parliament was dissolved on February 6, 1690, and Isaac Newton's official term there was at an end. He journeyed back to his college duties.

For two years Newton experimented with thermometers and studied the freezing and boiling points of water. He involved himself in his favorite pastimes, chemistry and Bible history, but he was not content.

The *Principia* was in print, and the challenge of Parliament was over. The sudden letdown in Newton's life brought a strange depression.

"A restlessness possesses me," Newton wrote to Halley. "I cannot sleep at night."

Overtired and overworked for years, Isaac Newton was suffering a nervous breakdown. "What lies ahead for me?" he cried in despair during months of illness in 1693.

What could possibly come after the *Principia*, a book that changed the world?

14. Guardian of the Mint

Isaac Newton opened his eyes and sat upright in bed. It was a spring morning in May 1694. Some students were singing by the fountain in Great Court.

Newton rose and swiftly dressed himself. God be praised! He was feeling better at last.

Once again, Trinity scholars saw his familiar figure in the lecture hall. Old Newton was just the same, the students decided.

His Cambridge friends were not so sure. What was this strange idea he had of obtaining a government post?

With his illness over, Newton worried about his future. Writing the great *Principia* had drained his creative mind without fattening his pocketbook. Influential London acquaintances urged him to seek a position in that city.

Newton sat at his table and studied their letters.

"England owes you a post of honor for your great work," wrote John Locke, the famous philosopher.

"Seek public recognition now," advised practical Samuel Pepys of the Admiralty.

Newton glanced out the window towards his laboratory. It was almost time to tend the furnace there, he reminded himself. The fire must burn night and day for his new experiments with metals and acids.

If he took a government job in London, he would have less time for science. But perhaps it was time for a permanent change. Trinity College had never really been the same since Barrow's death in 1677.

Pushing aside a clutter of papers, Newton reached for his quill pen. Charles Montagu was an important man in English politics now. He would ask Montagu to advise him about a suitable government post.

"As a scientist, your place is in the university," worried Cambridge professors told Newton. "You are only fifty-two and at the height of your creative powers."

"Every bone in my body begs for a change," Newton explained. "Science is a constant struggle."

The *Principia* had been so successful that he was planning a second edition with corrections and the addition of new material. He was having difficulty developing a new theory of the moon's motion, however. It seemed to Newton that John Flamsteed, England's astronomer royal, was withholding information about his observations on positions of the moon. Newton was troubled by this.

Finally a letter from Montagu arrived, summoning him to London. Newton's spirits soared.

The king had appointed Montagu as chancellor of the exchequer. One of the chancellor's duties was raising money to support the wars with France.

England's currency was in a terrible condition, which made his task much harder, Montagu wrote. The gold and silver coins in circulation were so damaged and worn that foreign traders often refused to accept them as payment. Silver coins, especially, had lost their true value. Dishonest people kept slicing off small pieces.

Montagu believed that only a complete recoinage would solve the problem. To accomplish this, Newton's mathematical genius and skill with metals were needed. Therefore, the king was appointing Isaac Newton to be warden of the Royal Mint.

This was the change Newton yearned for. If England needed him at the Mint, he believed it was his public duty to be there. He need not even give up the Lucasian Professorship. Another Cambridge mathematician offered to substitute while Newton was away.

As soon as Newton was established at the Mint quarters in the Tower of London, Montagu arrived to explain his vast new plan for recoinage.

"The old handmade coins are being called in over a period of time," Montagu began. "New coinage will, at the same time, be distributed."

"With a guaranteed amount of precious metal in each coin, I presume?" Newton asked.

The chancellor nodded. "We must restore the English people's confidence in their currency." He tossed his friend a shiny new shilling. "What do you think of this trial piece, Newton?"

"Beautiful," Newton murmured, examining the silver coin's machine-milled rim. He held it in his palm, estimating the weight.

"H'mm, 93 grains or so of metal," he announced. He pulled an old shilling from his money pouch. "Compared with only 50 grains in this damaged coin," he said.

"How can you be so certain?" Montagu asked, puzzled.

Isaac Newton smiled. "Years of scientific training, Charles. My fingers are educated. So are my eyes."

"The new coins will be like this silver shilling," the chancellor continued. "That is, they'll be uniform in size and with ornamented edges made by a secret process. This should prevent 'clippers' from chipping off bits of silver to reshape, with cheap metal, into counterfeit coins."

Isaac Newton listened carefully as Montagu outlined the plans. Recoinage would be no easy business. "We must think of the common people when we call in the old money," Newton remarked. "There must always be enough coins in circulation for wages and market money."

Montagu agreed. "And that, my friend, will be your responsibility."

Under Newton's skillful direction, more than 120,000 pounds of silver were stamped into new coins each week until the money emergency was over. His reputation for honesty and his scientific skill helped the English people have faith in their government during this critical time.

"No bribes shall corrupt me," Newton assured the citizens. He restored the practice of strict accuracy in coining money. Double records were kept of all transactions.

Newton's quarters at the Royal Mint were located at the Tower of London (below).

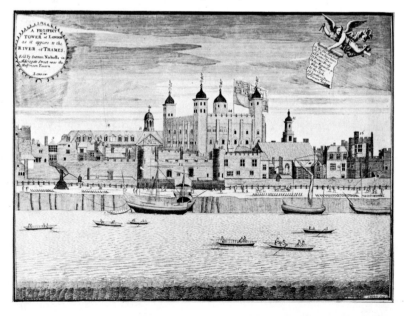

"You have become an excellent administrator, Newton," Montagu told him a year later. The two friends sat talking in the warden's garden. "The recoinage was efficiently done. Moreover, you've learned how to handle your employees very well."

Newton hesitated a moment before answering. "It's true, Charles. I've come to like working with people. And I enjoy London."

In 1699 Newton was promoted to be master of the Mint. He now sent for his seventeen-year-old niece, Catherine Barton, to take care of his new home near Piccadilly Square.

Poets would write sonnets to Catherine's beauty; statesmen would admire her wit. To Isaac Newton, however, Catherine was simply his half-sister Hannah's girl—a cheerful young person with dark ringlets framing a pretty face.

Catherine soon had the servants hanging curtains and polishing silver. Floors were rubbed with wax; windows were washed; beds were made up with snowy white sheets.

Newton watched the activity with amazement. "It's certainly grander than my quarters at Cambridge," he declared. "Who would think two human beings needed so many towels and cups and spoons and shelves?"

In 1701 the last Cambridge ties were broken when Newton resigned as Lucasian Professor of Mathematics. London had become home for Isaac Newton and his favorite niece.

Although his miraculous flood of new ideas was over, Newton was still England's great man of science. During this period he brought out plans for an improved sextant, an instrument needed for navigation at sea. Besides his work at the Mint, he served as advisor on scientific studies at Cambridge University. He continued to study moon motion, and he read widely in history and religion.

Perhaps the thing that delighted Newton most was being elected president of the Royal Society in 1703. For twenty-four years he was reelected annually to this post of honor.

Under Newton's able leadership the organization grew stronger. "It is a feather in my cap to have secured the membership of Prince George, husband to the Queen," he told a friend. Newton donated expensive equipment to the Society and gave demonstrations of the melting of metals.

Most important of all, Newton took time with young people. He encouraged promising young scientists with his friendship and good advice. His purse was always open for hungry students.

Robert Hooke had died in 1703. Safe now from further quarrels with his old rival, Newton published *Opticks*, his great work on the science of light. *Opticks* was recognized immediately as an important scientific achievement. It was far easier to understand than the difficult *Principia*, and the volume became a favorite of poets as well as scientists.

Isaac Newton now found himself in a new controversy. *Opticks* included his first complete explanation of his system of calculus. Word soon reached him that the German mathematician Leibniz was claiming credit for the invention.

"I value friends more highly than mathematical discoveries," Newton had once written to Leibniz. He tried, therefore, not to get involved in this quarrel. Outraged admirers, however, insisted that he must publish the truth for all the world to know. Newton's system of fluxions dated back almost forty years, they said. His Trinity lectures had touched on it. His letters to Collins and Barrow had mentioned it. So wasn't it Leibniz who had copied from Newton? they asked.

What could have been a simple misunderstanding between two brilliant minds became an international crisis. Both England and Germany felt their country's honor was at stake. No one stopped to think that each man had probably made an independent discovery. Newton had undoubtedly invented calculus many years before Leibniz, but Leibniz had been first to publish his own system.

Meanwhile, great public praise came to Newton. Earlier, the French Academy of Sciences had elected him to membership. Now in April 1705, he was knighted in a ceremony at Cambridge.

Students, professors, and townspeople lined the Cambridge streets to see Queen Anne and the Royal Court pass through Trinity's Great Gate. Happy voices cheered the glittering company.

In the reception room of the Master's lodge, 62-year-old Isaac Newton knelt before the queen. He felt the royal sword touch his shoulders. He heard the queen say, "It is a happiness to have lived at the same time as . . . so great a man."

From that day forward, the country boy from Lincolnshire would be known as Sir Isaac Newton.

Years were passing swiftly now, but Newton's brilliance had not dimmed. In the custom of the times, mathematicians frequently challenged each other to a kind of mathematical duel. In none of these was Sir Isaac Newton ever outmatched.

Sir Isaac Newton's house in London

Once Bernoulli, the celebrated Swiss mathematician, devised a difficult problem. He challenged anyone to find the answer within six months. Weeks sped by, and mathematicians remained baffled. Leibniz himself petitioned for an extension of the time.

Somehow eight months had already passed before Newton even heard about the challenge. Exhausted after a long working day, Newton attacked the problem directly after supper. Using his own system of calculus, he reached the solution in one sitting. By 4 A.M. he had prepared a copy, without his name attached, to be forwarded to Bernoulli.

The Swiss mathematician studied the papers. "The anonymous winner is England's Sir Isaac Newton," Bernoulli announced. "I can recognize the lion by his paw."

In 1716 Leibniz himself sent out a challenge. It was an unusual problem, one that the brilliant German believed would surely trap his 74-year-old rival.

Sir Isaac Newton solved it in one day. The English "lion" was still considered the world's great mathematician.

15. Father of the Space Age

In 1722, Sir Isaac Newton celebrated his eightieth birthday. The passing years had brought him fame and wealth, but the order of his days was much the same. He liked to waken early, spending the morning hours in quiet reading and writing. At night the lamps in his study still burned late.

Only special friends were invited into his favorite book-lined room. His little grandniece was always welcome there. Catherine had married John Conduitt, a wealthy member of Parliament, in 1717, but the Conduitts and their young daughter continued to live with Isaac Newton.

"I could not manage without you," Newton appealed to them. "And I am extremely fond of your child's company."

During these last years much of Newton's interest was devoted to the study of the Bible. He believed that there was a natural order in the universe—a design established by God.

"He is hardly ever alone without a pen in his hand and a book before him," John Conduitt often remarked. "Why can't the old gentleman take things easier!" Acting as Newton's deputy at the Mint, Conduitt lightened the scientist's duties.

Catherine presided over her uncle's three-story residence on fashionable St. Martin Street, just off Leicester Square. She was a popular hostess, noted for her charm and wit. To this new house came a steady stream of visitors—friends from the Royal Society, English statesmen, and distinguished foreigners who traveled long distances to see the great scientist. The *Principia* and *Opticks* had made Newton internationally famous.

At eighty, Sir Isaac Newton still enjoyed good health. His thick hair was pure white, but fresh, pink cheeks gave him a youthful look. His hearing was excellent, and he never wore spectacles. Friends often heard him boast of having kept all of his teeth but one!

Though Sir Isaac entertained in style, he himself preferred simple food and drink. He gave up tobacco because, as he said, he "would not be dominated by a habit."

Newton was still president of the Royal Society. Flurries of debate sometimes swirled about him, but few men dared attack his leadership. He was alert and full of ideas.

Catherine knew, however, that her uncle's absentmindedness increased each year. She watched carefully to save him from embarrassment. Once, several years earlier, something happened that even her thoughtfulness could not prevent.

Dr. William Stukeley had been invited one night to supper. Catherine arranged the food on the table, then left the two men to enjoy each other's company. Sir Isaac excused himself for a moment and went to the cellar to fetch a bottle of wine. Minutes passed and he did not return. Dr. Stukeley waited impatiently for an hour. Finally hunger overcame the doctor's good manners. He ate up the entire dinner, his own share and that of his host.

Newton returned at last, apologizing to his guest.

"I secured the wine," Newton explained, "but then began to think of something else. I remembered to return only because hunger gripped me." Sir Isaac stared in amazement at what remained of the supper. "How very strange," he said. "I thought I had not dined, but now I see I have."

That story quickly became part of the many Newton legends.

Late in 1722 an attack of illness warned that the years of good health were over.

"Fewer visitors and more rest," ordered Dr. Mead. "You must give up your coach, Sir Isaac. The jolting is bad for you. I am prescribing broth, vegetables, and fruit. No meat!"

He inspected his old friend's swollen ankles. "And get off your feet."

"Use legs, have legs," Newton reminded the physician. So long as he could walk about, he intended to do so.

A move to the village of Kensington was recommended. Perhaps the fresher country air would ease Newton's inflamed lungs. Reluctantly, the aged scientist packed his precious books and writing supplies and rented a house with a garden.

Sir Isaac Newton

Newton knew that time was on the wing. He selected Henry Pemberton, a brilliant young mathematician, to help him plan the third edition of the *Principia*.

Isaac Newton missed London. "Though he found the greatest benefit from rest and the air at Kensington . . . ," John Conduitt said, "no methods that we used could keep him from coming sometimes to town."

On February 28, 1727, Newton made his last trip to London to preside over the Royal Society meeting on March 2. He traveled by coach, jolting over miserable roads. The journey proved too fatiguing, and Newton never recovered. Early in the morning hours of March 20, death came to the eighty-four-year-old scientist.

The nation that had honored Isaac Newton in life paid him great tribute now. His body lay in state in Westminster Abbey and was buried there near England's kings.

Inscribed on his tomb are the words:

Let mortals rejoice
That there has existed such and so great
An Ornament of the Human Race

More than anyone before him, Isaac Newton used a pattern of investigation that we call the "scientific method of research." Experiment was his tool to observe, measure, record, and draw conclusions. He insisted on a finished, perfect product, and he worked with infinite patience to achieve his dreams.

Pioneer in astrophysics, first modern scientist, mathematical physicist—Newton was all of these. His accomplishments include the general binomial theorem, calculus, great advances in optics, the reflecting telescope, the law of universal gravitation, and Newton's laws of motion. He was a bold new thinker who brought science out of the Middle Ages.

Modern science builds on the platforms of his discoveries. More than 300 years after his birth, Newton's work makes new advances possible. Without it, the space age could not have dawned.

On Christmas Day 1968, Apollo 8 was homeward bound after man's first journey into the orbit of the moon.

"Who's driving up there?" asked an astronaut's young son in Mission Control at Houston, Texas.

Down from the spacecraft came his father's answer: "I think Isaac Newton is doing most of the driving right now."

Index